—THE GREAT BOOK OF—

CARS

Library of Congress Cataloging in Publication Data

Rutland, Jonathan.
The great book of cars.

Includes index.
SUMMARY: Describes cars through the years, including classic cars, racing cars, and cars of the future.
1. Automobiles—History—Juvenile literature.
[1. Automobiles—History] I. Cohen, Catherine.
II. Title.
TL147.R83 1981 639.2'222'09 81-759
ISBN 0-86592-062-1 AACR2

Pages 2 and 3: A racing car in the Monaco Grand Prix.

Opposite: A Bugatti sports car.

—THE GREAT BOOK OF—

CARS

RAY ROURKE PUBLISHING COMPANY, INC
WINDERMERE, FLORIDA 32786

Contents

Editorial

Author Jonathan Rutland

Designer Keith Groom

Editor Catherine Cohen

Published by Ray Rourke Publishing Company, Inc.
Windermere, Florida 32786.

Cars

Before the invention of railroads and motor cars, people did not often leave their home villages or neighborhood. When they did, they traveled on foot, or by horse. The motoring era began less than 100 years ago, yet in that short space of time cars have completely changed our lives. As fast motor transport became common, the pace of life quickened dramatically. Cars are now an essential means of transport. We think nothing of driving long distances to go to work, or just to go shopping or visit friends, and we may even motor across several countries on vacation.

Cars have brought more fun and freedom into our lives. They have also brought problems — in safety, pollution and traffic jams. Since the first few "horseless carriages" appeared transport has been revolutionized. This book tells the story of the transformation, describes many classic cars, explains how they work, and looks at the future of the motor car.

1909 Model T Ford

Strange Beginnings

Clockwork and Windmills

The picture above shows a sailing wagon built in the Netherlands in 1599. It was probably the first self-propelled road vehicle, but needing a following wind and a smooth road, it had no practical use. Other inventors experimented with kite-power, and even with windmills. Clockwork power seemed another possibility, but modern science has shown that wind-up cars are doomed to failure. A mainspring big enough to produce the power needed for a 32-km (20-mile) journey at 16 km/h (10 mph) would weigh five tons, and winding it would take hours.

Today cars are an essential part of our world, and it is hard to imagine life without them. Yet when the first cars were built few people could see any use for them. Inventive minds had dreamed for centuries of powered vehicles, but for most people travel meant going on foot or by horse. However, the spread of the railroads in the 19th century increased people's interest in travel. In the 18th century most roads were merely muddy tracks, and would not have been good enough for cars. In the 1820s John McAdam began building the best roads since Roman times, but there was still no practical engine for a car.

► Cugnot's steam gun carriage of 1769. It could travel at about 5 km/h (3 mph), but had to stop frequently to build up more steam.

Cars

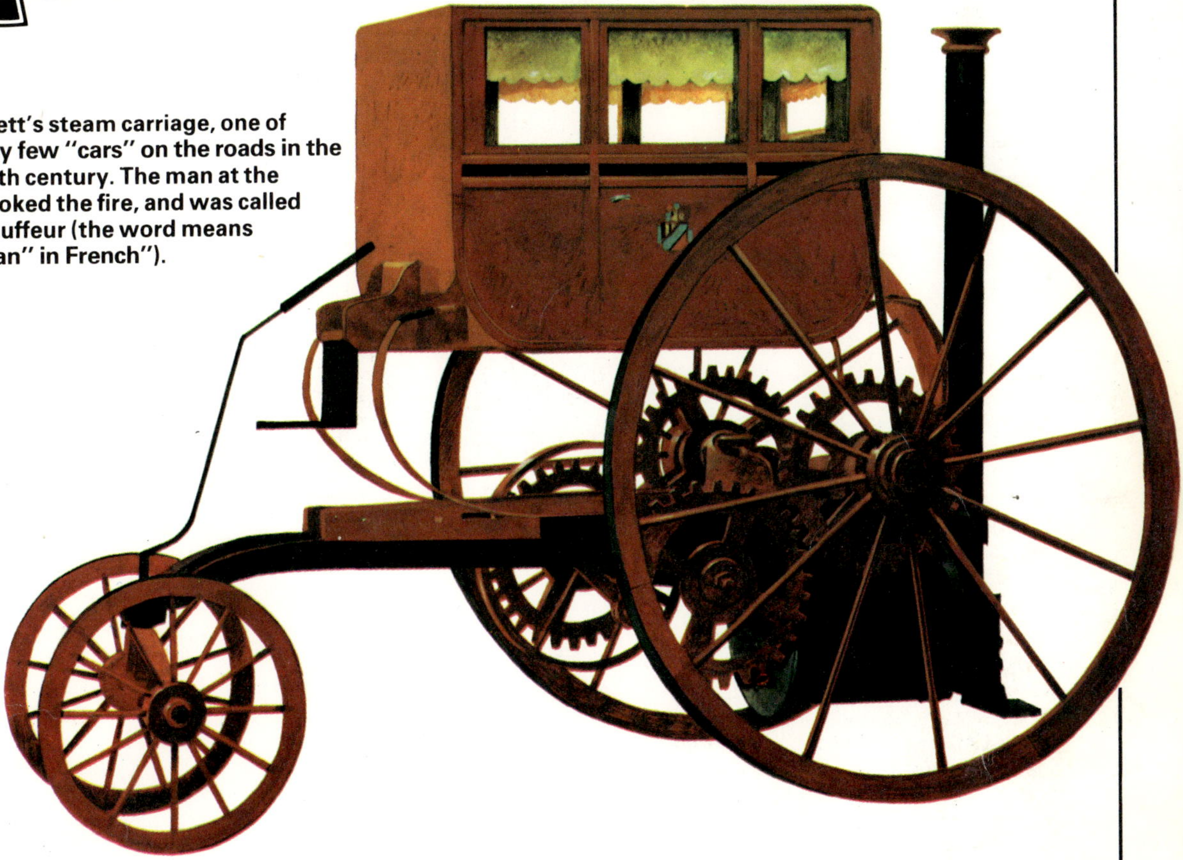

◄ Rickett's steam carriage, one of the very few "cars" on the roads in the mid-19th century. The man at the back stoked the fire, and was called the chauffeur (the word means "fireman" in French").

▲ Richard Trevithick's second steam carriage. Built in 1803, it travelled at 19 km/h (12 mph). However it aroused no interest.

Early attempts to build self-propelled vehicles without engines are described on the left. The true automobile had first to await the invention of an engine. First in the field was the steam engine, which transforms the heat from a coal or wood fire into mechanical energy for turning wheels.

The French engineer Nicholas Cugnot became the first man to construct a steam-powered road vehicle. Finished in 1769, it was a three-wheeled gun carriage. With a huge boiler ahead of the front wheel, it proved difficult to control, and finally crashed into a wall. Although hardly a workable vehicle, it was a start, and other inventors soon followed Cugnot's lead. The most successful was the English inventor, pioneer of steam railways, Richard Trevithick. His steam cars of 1801 and 1803 were the world's first truly practical cars. The first, nicknamed Captain Dick's Puffer, climbed a steep hill in Trevithick's home village, while the second, a small coach carrying eight passengers, steamed through the streets of London to the amazement and alarm of onlookers. There followed a brief era of steam coaches, but they were forced off the roads by competition from the railroads and horse-drawn carriages. Cars did not become popular for over fifty years.

The Horseless Carriage

◀ The first really commercially successful car, Karl Benz's Motorwagen of 1885. Unlike his principal rival, Daimler, Benz designed his vehicle as a whole, with a lightweight frame and wire-spoked bicycle-type wheels.

▶ This elegant Peugeot of 1896 still bears resemblances to its ancestor, the horseless carriage, with cart-type wheels, and the driver sitting unprotected in front of the luxurious passenger compartment.

▼ Gottlieb Daimler's first car, of 1886. Daimler, like most early horseless carriage builders, with the exception of Benz, concentrated his efforts on the engine, and then fitted it to a vehicle designed to be horse-drawn.

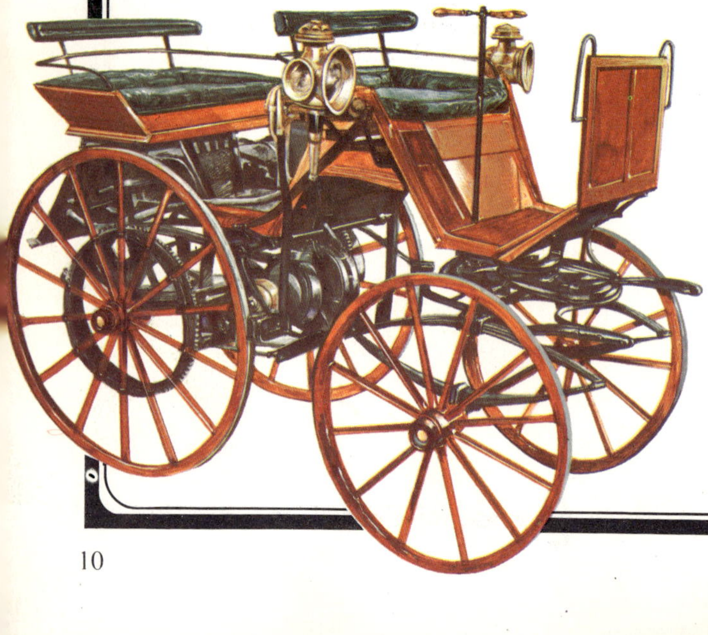

Motoring Firsts

- The world's first motor show was held in Tunbridge Wells, England, in 1895. Just five cars were on display.
- The first motor race also took place in 1895, in France. The winner averaged 24 km/h (15 mph) over the 1180 km (730-mile) course from Paris to Bordeaux and back, and drove through the night with the help of candles and oil lamps.
- 1896 was the year of the first electric starter, the first four cylinder car engine (a Panhard-Levassor), and of Henry Ford's first car. It was the only car in his home town of Detroit, and for security he chained it to a lampost when he left it unattended.
- 1898 was the year of the first fully enclosed car, a Renault.

◀ Benz's Viktoria demonstrating its abilities at the London Motor show of 1898. The Viktoria was first introduced in 1893.

▼ Benz's three-wheeler of 1888, the first car to be advertised and sold as a standard model. Few were actually sold, but its production marks the start of the motor industry. The car could travel at 19 km/h (12 mph).

The early steam cars suffered from several disadvantages. They were heavy and difficult to start. They seemed alarming — people did not like the idea of driving around with a furnace on board. All these problems were later overcome, but before that happened a new type of engine had appeared, fueled at first by coal gas and later by gasoline. This was the internal-combustion engine, or — as it was called by one early inventor — the explosion motor. In it a spark is used to explode gas or gasoline vapor inside a cylinder. The explosion forces the piston down the cylinder, and the piston's movement is used to turn wheels.

A Belgian, J.J. Lenoir, built the first internal-combustion engined car in Paris in 1862. It was fueled by coal gas, and took two hours to complete a 9-km (6-mile) trip through Paris. In 1875 the Austrian engineer, Siegfried Marcus, constructed a slightly more efficient gasoline-engined car. Lenoir and Marcus did not develop their ideas but other inventors, notably Benz and Daimler, worked to improve the gasoline engine, and to fit it in a practical road vehicle.

▼ This De Dion Bouton of 1901 was called a vis-à-vis, or face-to-face. It was an advanced car with shaft drive instead of the usual belt or chain.

Experimental Engines

▼ The French Scotte Steam Wagonette, an impressive steamer of the 1890s. But raising steam took over 30 minutes, and top speed was only 12 km/h (7½ mph).

Gas, Steam

The engines of all early cars were experimental, and all had problems. Steam-car owners had to wait while the boiler raised steam. Those with gasoline cars often had to light burners or adjust wicks (these were the forerunner of the spark plug). They then had to start the engine with a handle — a tough and sometimes dangerous job. Gradually engines were improved, but experiments continued and still do.

The flash boiler was an early invention to improve the steam car. The boiler was a coiled tube heated by paraffin burners. It turned water to steam in a flash, and with it, steamers of 1900-1920 were in many ways better than their gasoline-engined rivals. They were smoother, quieter and easier to drive. Today manufacturers are still experimenting with steam cars, particularly as they produce

▼ An experimental gas-turbine car of 1954. The streamlined shape was designed for speed, and the car reached 249 km/h (155 mph).

& Electricity

less exhaust fumes than gasoline cars. Expense remains the main problem. Electric cars were particularly popular in the early days, being the simplest, quietest and smoothest of all. But they had, and still have, one major disadvantage. Their power comes from batteries, and after 80 km (50 miles) or so these need recharging. The search is on for longer lasting batteries. In 1979 Volkswagen built an experimental electric car able to cruise for 160 km (100 miles) at 96 km/h (60 mph), and costing about half as much to run as a gasoline car.

The gas-turbine engine provides another possibility. In this the 'explosions' are used to spin a turbine, instead of driving pistons up and down. The result is a lighter and smoother running engine, but one that burns a lot of fuel.

▲ The Pope-Waverley was an American electric car of 1905. Its batteries only held enough power for about 48 km (30 miles), but the car was ideal as a town runabout, for shopping and going to work.

► During World War 2 gasoline was in short supply, and some people used household gas as fuel. In this car it is carried in a gas bag on the roof. Larger vehicles towed a gas generator.

The Parts of a Car

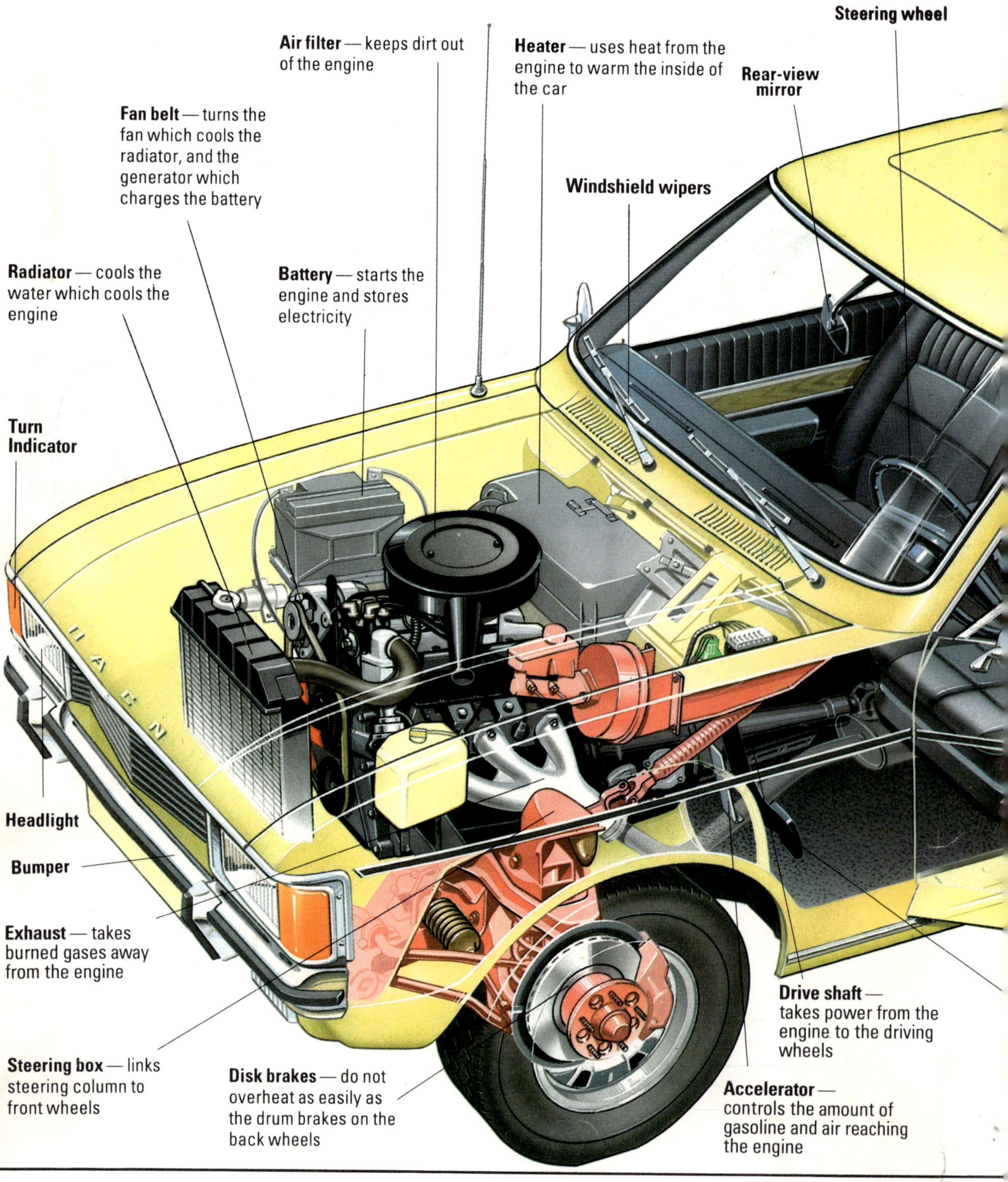

Motoring

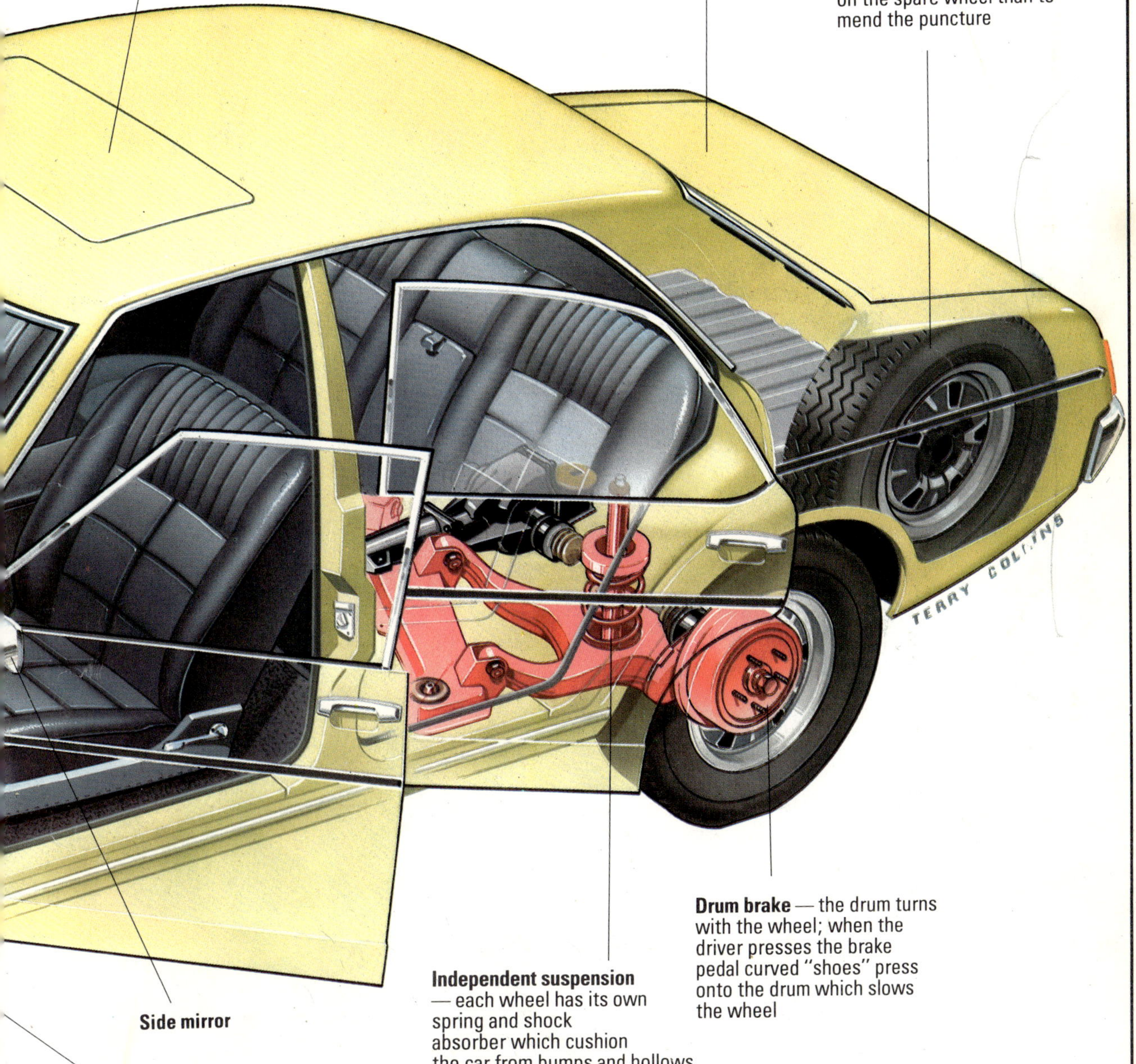

Sliding roof

Trunk

Spare wheel — when a tire punctures, it is easier and quicker to put on the spare wheel than to mend the puncture

Drum brake — the drum turns with the wheel; when the driver presses the brake pedal curved "shoes" press onto the drum which slows the wheel

Independent suspension — each wheel has its own spring and shock absorber which cushion the car from bumps and hollows in the road

Side mirror

Brake pedal — brakes equally on all wheels

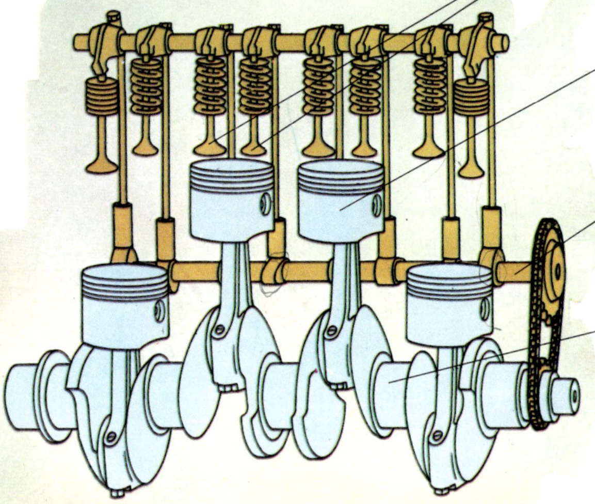
Rocker shaft
Valves
Piston
Camshaft
Crankshaft

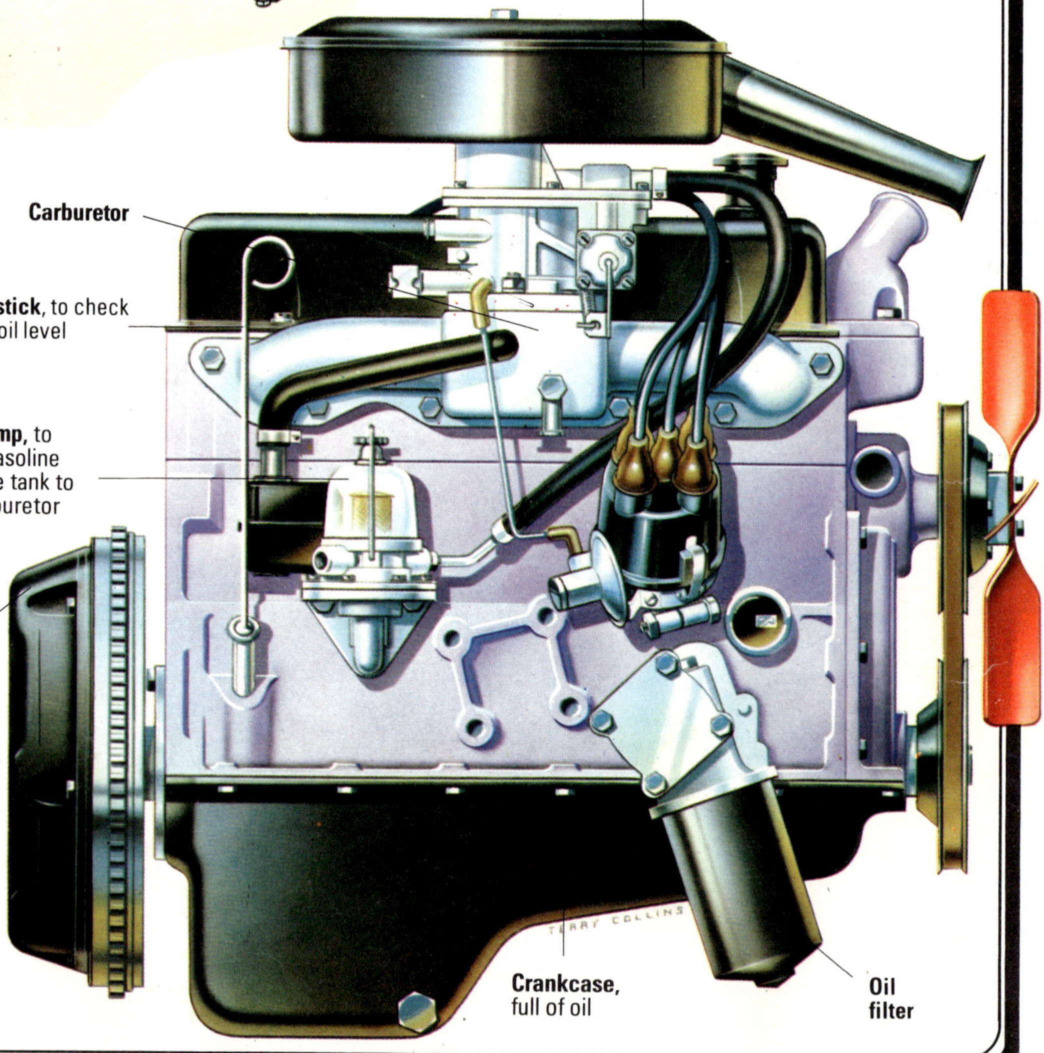
Air filter
Carburetor
Dipstick, to check the oil level
Fuel pump, to pump gasoline from the tank to the carburetor
Flywheel — heavy wheel fixed to the crankshaft to help the engine run smoothly
Crankcase, full of oil
Oil filter
TERRY COLLINS

Under the Hood

The heart of a car is its engine which consists of thousands of separate pieces and may have as many as 150 moving parts. The most important of these are the cylinders and pistons. The piston fits snugly inside the cylinder. There are usually four cylinders and pistons in a car but the number may vary from two up to twelve in a large car.

Most cars have four-stroke engines — the piston goes through two up-strokes and two down-strokes. First the inlet valve opens and as the piston moves down it draws in the gas-air mixture from the carburetor. Next the piston moves up compressing the mixture (squeezing it into a smaller space). This makes it explode more efficiently in the next stroke when a spark from the spark plug sets fire to the mixture. The explosion forces the piston down and turns the crankshaft which powers the car's driving wheels. The up-and-down movements of the pistons turn the crankshaft in much the same way as a cyclist's legs drive a bicycle chain. Lastly the exhaust stroke starts when the exhaust valve opens, the piston rises, and the burned gases are pushed out into the exhaust system. The sound of the explosions is reduced by the muffler. The whole cycle occurs repeatedly at great speed in each cylinder, which keeps the crankshaft turning.

Apart from the cylinders and their parts some of the other important bits of an engine are:

The starter motor, which draws electric power from the battery and spins the crankshaft. The engine the "fires" and continues running on its own.

The generator, which generates electricity when the engine is running, and keeps the battery charged.

The ignition coil, which increases the voltage (pressure of electricity) flowing from the battery to the distributor.

The distributor, which distributes electric power to each of the sparking plugs in turn.

The spark plugs, one to each cylinder, which explode the gas-air mixture by a spark.

Pumps: the fuel pump, which pumps gas from the fuel tank to the carburetor; the oil pump, which circulates oil through the lubrication system; the water pump, which helps water to circulate in the cooling system.

The carburetor, which sprays a mixture of gas and air into the cylinders.

TRANSMISSION

The transmission enables the driver to use the engine's power in the most efficient way. A car engine works best at a greater speed than the road wheels ever reach. If the engine did not run so fast it could not produce enough power to move the car. So the car has gears between the engine and the road wheels. Gears are devices which control the relationship between the power of the engine and the speed of the car.

Gears consist of toothed wheels of different sizes which mesh together. In the example here the smaller wheel moves faster than the larger, but the big slow-turning wheel has the greater turning power.

In cars with manual transmission the driver changes gear by moving a lever attached to the gearbox and pressing the clutch pedal which disconnects the engine. He chooses low gear when he needs most power but little speed, i.e. when starting or climbing a steep hill. The driver chooses higher gears to make the car move faster for the same range of engine speeds. In many cars the gears change automatically.

Cars for Everyone

At first, motoring was an adventure, one only the wealthy could afford, and one only the hardy and mechanically minded wanted to risk. Apart from frequent breakdowns, pioneer motorists had to deal with attacks from dogs, pedestrians and farmers. But when cars became cheaper and more reliable, more people wanted to drive. Some manufacturers concentrated on quality and luxury. Until 1906 Mercedes were reckoned the best cars in the world, but in that year their place was taken by Rolls Royce. The Silver Ghost's engine was so quiet that you could hear the clock ticking, and so sturdy and reliable that after a 24,140-km (15,000-mile) test drive it needed virtually no attention. The most famous of the cheaper cars was the Model T Ford, popularly known as Tin Lizzie. Simple and robust, designed to go anywhere, the Model T was an instant success.

▼ A scene from the early 1900s. Like most cars of the time, this runabout had no cab to protect occupants from the weather and from dust and mud thrown up from the road. Clothing firms produced special motoring wear, with fashionable silk hoods for women, caps and goggles for men, and leather or fur outfits for bad weather.

◄ The first Rolls Royce, the Silver Ghost of 1906. It cruised at well over 80 km/h (50 mph), and later models reached over 130 km/h (80 mph).

◀ One of the world's first mini cars, the French Bébé Peugeot of 1913. Designed by Ettore Bugatti, later famous for his racing and luxury cars, it was the smallest four-cylinder car of its time. Racing Bébés and enclosed coupé versions were also made.

▼ One of Britain's first mini cars, the Baby Austin of 1922. It was designed as a big car in miniature, to appeal to family motorists, and could carry two adults and two children. The standard model cruised at 72 km/h (45 mph), but racing models were almost twice as fast.

▲ From 1908 until 1927 Ford built just one type, the Model T. But it came in a wide range of versions, from a tiny Doctor's Buggy to a tractor, a racing car, and the 1923 Fordor Sedan shown here.

▶ One of the early Model T Fords, a Tin Lizzie of 1909. It was cheap to run, easy to maintain, and had a top speed of about 64 km/h (40 mph).

◀ A solid British family car of the 1920s and early 1930s, the Bullnose Morris. Morris studied American sales methods, and made this car a best seller.

During the 1930s, car manufacturers concentrated on making cars larger and more comfortable. They added refinements such as heaters, synchromesh transmission (which make gear-changing easier), and power-assisted brakes and steering, windshield washers, directional indicators, and seat belts. Most of these became standard equipment. During the 1930s some of the finest high-performance cars of all time were built by firms such as Bentley, Rolls Royce, Duesenberg, Cadillac, Bugatti and Hispano-Suiza. Many of the cars from this period are still in perfect running order. The years immediately before and after World War 2 saw a renewed interest in small economy cars, including the best seller ever, the Volkswagen Beetle.

Firsts

- Early car heaters were "Motor Hot Water Bottles". The first heater using heat from the engine appeared in the USA in 1926.
- Traffic lights first appeared in Detroit in 1919.
- Synchromesh gears first appeared in a 1929 standard production Cadillac. Vauxhall and Rolls Royce followed in Britain in 1932.
- In 1922 Ford became the first firm to build over a million cars in one year. This was equalled by Volkswagen in 1962, and by British Leyland in 1968.
- 1936 was the year of the first diesel-engined private car, a Mercedes-Benz. Diesels are cheaper to run and more reliable than gas engines, but cost more, are noisier, and have less acceleration.
- An important step forward in safe motoring was the opening of the first super highway, in Italy in 1924. Germany followed in 1935, the US in 1940, and Britain in 1958.

◀ A late model of the Volkswagen Beetle. When production stopped in 1978, 19¾ million had been made — a record.

The 30s and After

and Feats

• Citroen introduced front-wheel drive and unit construction (with body and chassis in one unit) as early as 1934. The picture below shows their revolutionary DS 19 of 1955, with advanced streamlining and hydro-pneumatic suspension. This keeps the car level, and allows the driver to raise and lower the entire car to suit the road surface.

▲ A Jaguar XK 120 of 1950, one of the most famous sports-racers ever made. It won race after race, was a popular road car, and had a top speed of 212 km/h (130 mph).

▲ A 1957 Cadillac. Huge fins and grilles were popular in the 1950s.

▼ This supercharged Duesenberg SJ of 1934 was popular with film stars and gangsters in the US, and with kings and queens in Europe. Its top speed was 208 km/h (128 mph).

Cars

For years car manufacturers tried to produce ever bigger and faster cars, and the cost of buying and running them continued to rise. This was especially true in the U.S., where huge cars with powerful engines, elaborate bodywork and all sorts of luxuries and gadgets have for long been popular. Today even here people have become more concerned about price and running costs, and the great American car manufacturers are designing smaller and more economical cars.

Around the world, cars being designed and built now are unlikely to be startlingly different in shape from those produced in recent years. They

▲ The Porsche Turbo. Porsche are a leading German firm making racing and sports cars. This model has a top speed around 242 km/h (175 mph). A turbo charged engine gives more power than a normal one.

▲ The Italian Fiat 125, one of the smallest cars on the road today.

▲ The Swedish Volvo 244 Gl incorporates many of the latest safety features.

▼ The wedge-shaped Italian Lamborghini Urraco, a streamlined coupé.

▲ The British Leyland Mini is surprisingly roomy for its size and is economical to run.

Rotary Power

Most car engines cause vibration and noise. A German engineer, Felix Wankel, invented an entirely new engine with only three moving parts, and they all rotate or turn. The result is a simple and smooth-running engine. The main advantage is that power is produced at every turn of the rotor, while only every fourth stroke of a piston is a power stroke. At the moment rotary engines burn too much fuel, but perhaps more and more cars of tomorrow will have rotary power.

Now

will be improved in details, and many more of the safety features described on pages 42-43 will soon be part of every car. They will also include other advanced ideas, including streamlining, and electronic ignition, and they will be more efficient, getting more power from less fuel, and causing fewer exhaust fumes. Some manufacturers are also working on ways of making cars easier and cheaper to service. This is achieved by designing the car so that all parts needing regular attention are easy to get at, by reducing the number of parts needing servicing, and by simplifying the work involved. But we are far from designing the perfect car.

▲ The Ford Fiesta, a typical small hatchback family car. Great care was taken to make it easy to maintain and economical.

▲ The Italian Ferrari Boxer, a high performance car with many new features including a mid-engine layout. This gives excellent roadholding and balance. The 5-liter 12-cylinder engine gives a top speed of around 290 km/h (180 mph).

▼ The Rover SDI, one of the most successful new cars on the road. It has dual circuit brakes, a "crumple zone" at front and rear to cushion the main cab, and many other safety features.

Types of Car

SEDAN — the traditional family car. It has a fixed roof, a trunk, carries at least four people, and has four or two doors.
STATION WAGON — this is similar to a sedan but instead of having a trunk the main compartment extends to the back, to provide luggage space behind the rear seat. As with the hatchback, there is a rear door.
HATCHBACK — this has become very popular recently, and combines features of the sedan and station wagon. It has a fixed roof, carries at least four people, and has two or four doors in the sides. But it also has an extra door or "tail gate" at the back.
LIMOUSINE — a large and luxurious sedan. Many are chauffeur driven and have a glass partition between the driver and the passenger compartment.
CONVERTIBLE — a car with a roof that can be folded down or removed.
SPORTS CAR — a low and streamlined car for fast driving, and usually with only two seats.
COUPÉ — a small sedan, usually with only two seats and two doors.

How Cars are Made

Hand-made by Robots

Everyone makes mistakes, usually when they are tired or fed up. These mistakes may result in the "Monday morning car" — one badly assembled and full of faults.

Robots can be very useful in building cars. They work efficiently and are not troubled by doing repetitive work. Some car manufacturers in Japan and Italy use machines like the robot welders on the right. Robots are programed by computer to do many tasks which are dangerous to human beings. They move objects which are too hot or heavy for people to handle. Robots can work in places which are too hot or too cold for people, and are not affected by poisonous fumes. But if they break down, a human engineer must attend to the fault.

A new car is produced after careful planning by engineers, designers and sales people. The first steps in building a car, making the body, take place in a large factory away from the main assembly or production line. Huge sheets of steel are placed in massive presses which bend them into shape for the various parts of the body. The parts are next welded together to form the monocoque or unit body. "Mono" means "one" and "coque" means "shell". The body is now a single shell — unlike early cars, which were built up on a frame or chassis to which the body was added. The finished bodies are dipped in wax or grease for protection, and sent to the actual car factory. There they are dipped in baths for degreasing and rustproofing, and than after being rubbed smooth they go to the paint shop where they receive several coats of paint.

Many other parts in addition to the body arrive at the production line ready made. They include the carburetor, the transmission, the wiring "harness" (the maze of wires that carry electricity around the car), and often the entire engine. The production line consists of an extremely long and slow moving conveyor. The empty body is placed on the start of the line, and by the time it rolls off at the other end it is a finished car, ready for testing. Along the line about 150 men are stationed, each completing one part of the assembly as the growing car moves slowly past. Overhead conveyors bring the right parts to each "station", so the whole process needs much careful planning and organization. If just one person fails to complete his task, or if one part fails to arrive in time, the entire production line must stop. Even a brief halt wastes a lot of time and

▲ **Henry Ford pioneered the production line to speed up assembly, and allow him to lower prices. Here Model T bodies are lowered onto the chassis.**

◀ **At Volvo's factory at Kalmar in Sweden, the production line is replaced by movable platforms like this. The workers control its speed.**

▼ **A typical car production line in Japan. The parts and tools needed for each step are stacked on the racks.**

money. On some lines a finished car rolls off every couple of minutes, and in many factories the line is kept going day and night. As one team of workers leaves the next shift takes over.

Doing the same task over and over again all day as the line moves past is very boring, so some manufacturers, such as Volvo, are experimenting with ways to make car production more interesting for the workers. Volvo workers form groups and rotate the jobs among themselves. They are responsible for the speed and quality of the work they do. Other firms use robots to do the most dull and routine tasks.

When the car leaves the production line it is inspected for faults and given a waterproofing test. Every so often one car is given a thorough road test. After testing, the cars are ready for delivery.

Famous

Spectacular Cars

◀ This fantastic six-wheeler, a De Dietrich of 1903, was built for a baron, and cost five times as much as the standard model.

◀ This beautiful Peugeot vis-à-vis (face-to-face) was built in 1892 and earned the nickname of "Pearly Queen". It was decorated to look well with the fashionable clothes of the time, and must have needed an artist to maintain the paintwork.

or Fantastic

In the early days two quite separate firms were usually involved in building a car. One, the motor manufacturer, built the basic chassis, complete with engine and all other mechanical parts. Another, the coach-builder, added the bodywork, often to the customer's specification. So cars were much less standardized than today. They included specials with boat-shaped wooden bodywork, wickerwork bodies, and one built for an Indian prince with an ornate carriage in the style of earlier horse-drawn coaches. Another, shown top left, had wickerwork panels for decoration, and an elongated body carried on six wheels. The driver sat unprotected in the front. Behind him was a luxuriously equipped passenger compartment, while behind this was a kitchen where meals were prepared for the journey.

£ £ £ Expensive Cars $ $ $

Wealthy people pay enormous sums of money to have cars fitted out to their own specifications. Sometimes their money is spent solely on the appearance of the car. One example was the Gold Car built by Daimler for Lord and Lady Docker in 1951. Almost all the unpainted metal parts were gold-plated, including even the radio controls. Britain's most expensive production car is the Rolls Royce Carmargue. It costs about $136,000 — as much as a large house, yet some people are prepared to pay three times the basic cost for an armor-plated version. The most expensive car of all is the American president's official car, a Lincoln Continental built in 1968. Designed to protect the president from all possible danger, it carries two tons of armor plate, can travel at speed with all four tires punctured, and cost around $500,000.

► The Lincoln Continental Presidential limousine. Lincoln cars first earned their title "the car of presidents" in 1920.

▼ One of the most expensive and famous production cars in the world today, the Rolls Royce Corniche.

▶ **The Bugatti Royale, 1927. The largest production car of all time, it was over 6·7 m (22 ft) long, with a 2 m (7 ft) bonnet, and a 4·3 m (14 ft 2in) wheelbase. The 13-liter engine was so powerful that gears were hardly needed. Middle gear was used from 5 to 113 km/h (3 to 70 mph). First was just for starting, and third for speed — up to 190 km/h (120 mph). As it cost a small fortune ($30,000 for the chassis alone), the Royale was a commercial failure. But Bugatti was determined to make use of its massive engine and he adapted it to power high-speed rail cars. In over 30 years of car manufacture, Bugatti's factory built only about 7000 cars, but they were beautifully designed and superbly engineered, and many are still in perfect running order, the prized possessions of collectors and enthusiasts.**

Biggest and Smallest

The Italian car designer Ettore Bugatti decided to build a car which would be the biggest and best in the world. He had been told that his cars were the fastest, but Rolls Royce the best. He answered: "I will soon arrange to alter that," and set to work on the Bugatti Royale. It was a magnificent car, so well-made that Bugatti guaranteed each Royale for life. But it was too large and too expensive even for the Royal families Bugatti hoped would buy it, and only six were built. The largest car in the world is a "one off" Cadillac. It stretches to an

▲ **A German Messerschmitt bubble car of the 1960s. It carried two people, one behind the other, and looked rather like an aeroplane cockpit.**

▶ **The Ford Edsel of 1958, a great car for an unusual reason. It was the greatest financial flop. People did not like the huge grilles, and would not buy the Edsel. Fords had lost $250 million when production stopped in 1959.**

amazing 8·99 m (29·5 ft), and includes two TV sets, a bar, a refrigerator, and a safe.

At the other end of the scale come mini cars. These are most popular in times when people do not have much money. They are cheap to buy and to run. After World War 1 roughly built and often dangerous cycle cars were common. They had motor cycle engines, plywood bodies, and very crude brakes and steering. The period after World War 2 was the era of the bubble car.

When is a Car not a Car?

Inventors have played with countless weird ideas for cars. One even joined two 'half cars' together, to provide an engine and all controls at both ends. If the two drivers worked carefully together they could drive the car sideways. Another inventor constructed a two-wheeled "gyrocar", kept upright by gyroscopes (heavy spinning wheels inside the car), and there have been eight-wheelers, six-wheelers, and a five-wheeler (see far right).

◄ The Leyat aerocar, 1923. The propeller pulled it along at up to 80 km/h (50 mph). Steering was by the rear wheels, which must have been difficult.

▼ A steamlined car of the early 1920's, the Rumpler Tropfenwagen. It was efficient but unpopular.

▲ Several inventors have experimented with flying cars, and with amphibians. This flying car was made for the James Bond film "The Man With the Golden Gun".

► A strange twin-hulled racing car built in 1955, the Nardi Bisilure. The engine filled one hull, the driver sat in the other.

▼ **This swan car was built in 1912 by the Brooke Car Company. It even hissed like a swan.**

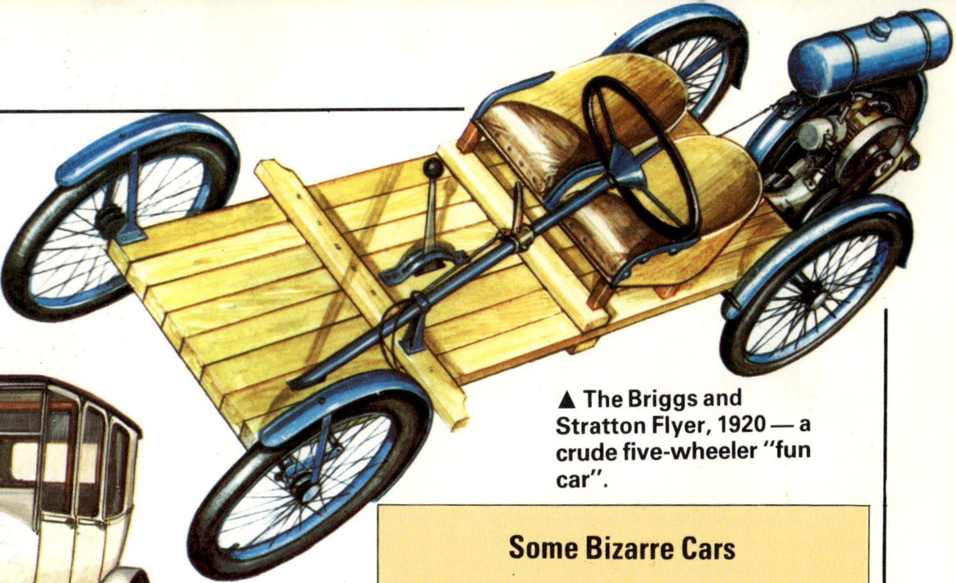

▲ **The Briggs and Stratton Flyer, 1920 — a crude five-wheeler "fun car".**

Some Bizarre Cars

Shown on these pages are some of the oddest cars ever made, but several had some practical value — even the mechanical horse, which was designed to bring the advantages of motoring without frightening animals or pedestrians. The Leyat aerocar was one of several attempts to use aircraft propulsion in cars. This was not a success unlike the boat-like Tropfenwagen. Its streamlined shape was designed to slip through the air as easily as possible — an idea that is becoming ever more popular today, for it increases speed and saves fuel. The swan, on the other hand, was made for an eccentric Englishman purely for fun. So was the five-wheeled Flyer, even though its makers claimed that it was "one of the most popular contrivances ever brought out for Young Americans". It had no gears, no suspension, and no clutch. The lawn mower engine turned the fifth wheel and gave a top speed around 40 km/h (25 mph).

▼ **This mechanical horse of 1897 was designed to pull carriages.**

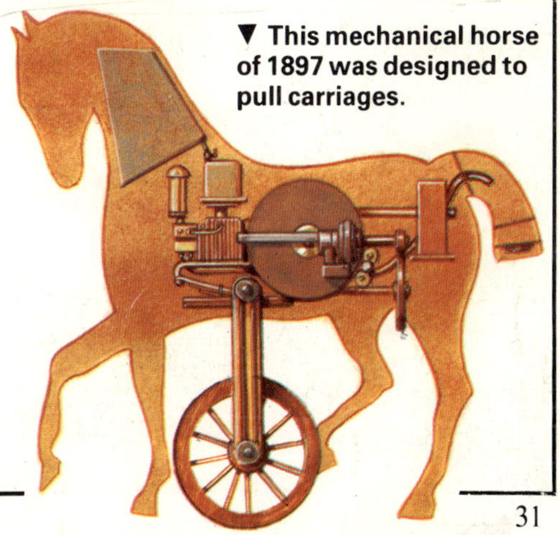

Special Purpose Cars

Custom Cars

Custom cars are vehicles which are built or altered to a customer's particular wishes. Customization has been popular since the early days of cars. A 1906 Renault town carriage was built 2·4 meters (8 feet) high because the owner liked to keep his top hat on. Today customization may involve using the chassis from one car, the front of a second car, the suspension systems of a third, while the engine may come from a fourth, and so on. The result will be a car which is quite unlike any other, and probably the pride of the owner's heart. The paintwork is often very jazzy, and may amount to "auto art" as in the artistically decorated car below. The resale value of the car is boosted by the professionalism of the designs. There are large numbers of custom car enthusiasts in England and the USA and they hold shows to exhibit their unique cars.

▲ *Stingray*, a special purpose fun car. It is deliberately driven in this nose-up position, and has tiny wheels at the back for balance. The driver sees ahead through a window in the floor. Despite its appearance, *Stingray* is not a racing car, but an exhibition car.

Top left: *Spirit of America-Sonic 1*, a car with just one purpose — to go as fast as possible along a straight and level course to break the world land speed record. It was driven by a jet engine like an airplane, and in 1965 it reached the amazing speed of 988.12 km/h (613.99 mph). This record has only been beaten by two cars.

► The most "special" of all, the Lunar Roving Vehicle or "moon buggy" used by American astronauts for exploring on the Moon. Powered by batteries, it had a top speed of 16 km/h (10 mph).

Some special purpose cars are designed to do just one very special task. These include the "moon buggy" illustrated, and the "orange car" built to advertise a firm that sold oranges. The car was orange-shaped.

At the other end of the scale are special purpose cars designed to tackle a variety of tasks. The best known of these are sturdy vehicles with four-wheel drive like Land Rovers and Jeeps. On most cars the engine turns only one pair of wheels. With four-wheel drive, it turns all four, thus giving an extra good grip and allowing the car to work on rough ground where a normal car would skid and get bogged down. An early version with the same purpose was driven along by caterpillar tracks like a tank, but had ordinary front wheels. Most other special purpose cars are built to break speed records, or to test new ideas.

Built for

Early Sports and Racing Cars

▲ An American racing car of 1906, the Locomobile Old 16. With a top speed of 177 km/h (110 mph), it was the first American racer able to compete with European rivals. In 1908 it provided the US with her first win in international racing during the Vanderbilt Cup.

▲ This early photograph shows Marcel Renault speeding at 129 km/h (80 mph) in the Paris-Madrid race shortly before he was killed.

► The Bugatti Type 35, the most successful Grand Prix racing car of all time, and the world's first standard production Grand Prix racer. In the years 1925-1927 Bugatti cars won almost 2000 races, while during the following three years the Type 35 won 14 of the most important international events.

Speed

► A futuristic pioneer of streamlining, built in Italy in 1913 and known as the torpedo car.

▲ The bizarre Lion-Peugeot during speed trials in 1911.

► A Mercedes-Benz Model S, one of the most popular sports cars of the 1920s.

Early Records

- The first races were as much a test of endurance as speed. Many failed to complete the course, or even to start. Over 100 cars entered for the first Reliability Trial, of 1894, but only 19 actually started.
- The winner of the first real race, from Paris to Bordeaux and back, in 1895, was Emil Levassor. He earned an all-time record for the longest racing drive — 48 hours and 48 minutes with hardly a break.
- Early racers were beset by many problems. The races were held on ordinary roads which were often rough and threw up clouds of blinding dust, and animals sometimes attacked the cars.
- The most deadly of all early races was the 1903 Paris-Madrid race. Spectators crowded onto the course. Dust filled the air, and drivers unable to see the road had to follow the tops of telegraph poles and trees. So many people were killed that the race, known as the Race of Death, was stopped.

The Racing World

After the Paris-Madrid "Race of Death", racing organizers decided that for safety, races should be held on closed circuits. Today most races are held on tracks such as Brands Hatch in England and Indianapolis in America. Others are run on ordinary roads, but they are sealed before the race and made as safe as possible for both spectators and drivers. Road circuits include the Monaco course around the streets of Monte Carlo, and the famous Le Mans circuit in France. This is the scene of an unusual kind of race, a 24-hour race. Here the winner is the one to travel the greatest distance in 24 hours.

▼ The Porsche 917, 1970. This was the fastest road racer ever (378 km/h, 235 mph), the most powerful production car, and the car with the fastest lap speed (260·85 km/h, 162·087 mph).

Until about 15 years ago, racing cars looked similar to ordinary sports cars. But in 1967 they sprouted "wings" and since then have grown ever more specialized and unlike normal cars. The wings, called airfoils or spoilers, work like upside-down airplane wings. Aircraft wings provide "lift" for flying. Racing car airfoils push the car down. This gives the wheels a better grip on the track.

The most important races are Grand Prix events. These international contests are for the most specialized of all racing cars, the Formula 1 cars. However there are plenty of events for more ordinary cars. They include autocross and rallycross, usually run over muddy fields, and rallies. Rallies take place on normal roads, and test driving skill and endurance rather than speed.

The red flag means that all cars must stop immediately.

The black flag is shown with the car number to tell the driver he must stop.

The blue flag warns a driver that another car is close behind.

▲ Drag cars like this race in pairs over a straight 400 m (¼ mile) drag strip, from a standing start.

▼ A Formula 1 Grand Prix car. This is the McLaren M26 which was driven by Britain's James Hunt in 1978.

◄ The Elf Tyrell 008. It was the car driven by Patrick Depailler when he won the 1978 Monaco Grand Prix.

Formula Rules

Each kind of race has its own set of rules and regulations. These are called the formula. The formula limits the size and weight of the cars and their engines, and specifies everything down to the last detail, including safety equipment, the length of the race, and the type of fuel. The kings of the race track, Formula 1 racers, are single seater cars with engines up to 3000 cc. Most have the same engine, the Cosworth-Ford, and average speeds during 250-km (155-mile) races are sometimes over 200km/h (124 mph).

The red and yellow flag warns drivers that the track is slippery.

The chequered flag is waved as the winner crosses the finishing line.

Record Breakers

▶ This bullet-shaped electric record breaker, *La Jamais Contente* (the never satisfied), was the first to reach 100 km/h (62 mph), in 1899, and it held the record for three years. A spectator at the record-breaking run said it sped along "with a subdued noise like the rustling of wings, scarcely seeming to touch the ground".

◀ The 1000-horsepower Sunbeam became the first car in the world to exceed 124 km/h (200 mph), in 1927. It was powered by two huge airplane engines, and was one of the first cars built especially for the land speed record.

▶ John Cobb set a new record in 1947 in this Railton, and briefly topped 643 km/h (400 mph).

Fastest in the World

		km/h	mph
1898	Jeantaud electric car	63·15	39·24
1899	Jenatzy's *La Jamais Contente*	105·88	65·79
1902	Serpollet steam car	120·80	75·06
1903	Gobron-Brillé	136·36	84·73
1904	Ford 999 (driven by Henry Ford)	147·05	91·37
1905	Napier	176·45	109·65
1906	Stanley steamer, the *Beetle*	195·65	121·57
1922	Sunbeam	215·25	133·75
1925	Sunbeam (M. Campbell)	242·80	150·87
1926	Sunbeam (Henry Segrave)	245·15	152·33
1927	Thomas Special	275·23	171·02
1927	Sunbeam (Henry Segrave)	327·97	203·79
1928	White-Triplex (R. Keech)	334·02	207·55
1919	*Golden Arrow* (Henry Segrave)	372·47	231·44
1931	Napier-Campbell (M. Campbell)	396·04	246·09
1932	Napier-Campbell (M. Campbell)	408·73	253·97
1935	Campbell Special (M. Campbell)	489·74	304·31
1937	*Thunderbolt* (G. Eyston)	502·12	312·00
1938	*Thunderbolt* (G. Eyston)	575·34	357·50
1939	Railton (J.R. Cobb)	594·97	369·70
1947	Railton (J.R. Cobb)	634·40	394·20
	The following were jet- or rocket-powered cars		
1963	*Spirit of America* (C. Breedlove)	655·73	407·45
1964	*Green Monster* (A. Arfons)	863·75	536·71
1965	*Spirit of America* — Sonic 1	988·12	613·99
1970	*Blue Flame* (G. Gabelich)	1016·09	631·37

In 1898 a Frenchman reached the then amazing speed of 63·15 km/h (39·24 mph) in an electric car. Many of the early record holders were electric and steam cars, and one, the Stanley steamer *Wogglebug*, became in 1907 the fastest vehicle on Earth. Hurtling along a beach in Florida, USA, it reached 241 km/h (150 mph) before hitting ridges in the sand and breaking up. Surprisingly no gasoline car has ever held this absolute speed record. Before *Wogglebug*, trains were fastest, while afterwards aircraft and then spacecraft have been the fastest vehicles of all.

The early record-breaking drivers were thought to face other dangers as well as accidents. Medical experts said they would not be able to breathe when traveling so fast, and that their hearts would stop. But today's drivers even break the sound barrier at speeds that were once unthinkable.

▲ The 21.7 liter Fiat *Mephistopheles*, a giant that broke the land speed record eight times between 1923 and 1925.

◀ *Blue Flame* attained the official world speed record of 1016 km/h (631 mph) in 1970. However, in December 1979, Stan Barrett driving a 60,000 horsepower rocket-powered vehicle reached the amazing speed of 1188km/h (739 mph).

Cars of

Towards Tomorrow

◀ The General Motors XP-883, an experimental car with both electric and gasoline power.

▼ The Comuta, an experimental electric town car, 1970.

Future Power

The ideal car engine would be quiet, cheap to run, and free from pollution. Electric cars come closest to this idea. Research is being carried out in many countries but designing a long-lasting battery remains a problem. Even so, before long, small electric cars will probably become popular, where journeys are short and the car can be plugged in at home each night to recharge the batteries. Another idea is for cars with both gasoline engine and electric motor. When the batteries run down, the petrol engine powers the car and charges the battery. Steam, diesel and gas turbine engines all have some advantages, but most cars will probably continue to be powered by gasoline engines in the near future.

the Future

For around the first 75 years of motoring, most firms concentrated on making cars more powerful, more luxurious, more full of gadgets, and more roomy. These points are still important, but recently the emphasis has changed. Fuel is increasingly expensive, and people now realize the dangers of pollution. So today car firms are trying to make cars quieter, cleaner, safer, and cheaper to run. They are working on systems to stop poisonous exhaust gases reaching the air; on ways to make engines more efficient; and on making the car body itself more efficient, more streamlined. The more easily a car slips through the air, the less the fuel needed to keep it moving. There are three basic streamlined shapes, the shark, the wedge and the box. The shark slopes down to a "knife-edge" at front and back. This is the most efficient shape, but it leaves little room inside. The wedge is pointed at the front but cut off straight at the rear, while the box, a blunt-nosed wedge, provides the roomiest car of the three.

◀ The Modulo, an experimental styling research vehicle built in 1969. It is only about 1 m (3 ft) high. Created by the famous Italian car design company Pininfarina, the Modulo is half way between the shark and wedge shapes, and has many futuristic features. The roof and windshield section slides forward for access. The headlights are set flush in the body for streamlining. there is an adjustable front airfoil (under the nose). And the car, which is built on a Ferarri chassis, has broad racing-style tires.

▶ Another styling research vehicle, the Ford Coin Car of 1974, is well streamlined. Like the Modulo above, it is a cross between wedge and shark, and has an adjustable front airfoil (at the top of the windshield).

Far left: The Ford Comuta's batteries provided a range of only about 24 km (15 miles) and a top speed of 56 km/h (35 mph). Batteries have now been improved to give nearly eight times the range and twice the speed.

Safety experts deliberately crash test cars with dummy people on board to help discover exactly what happens in a collision, and to research ways of making such accidents less disastrous.

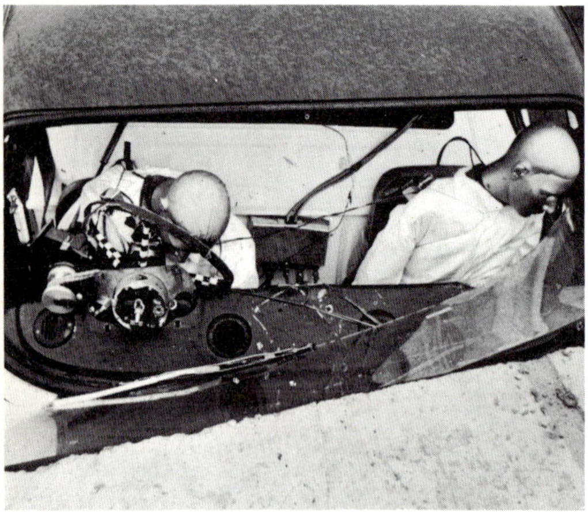

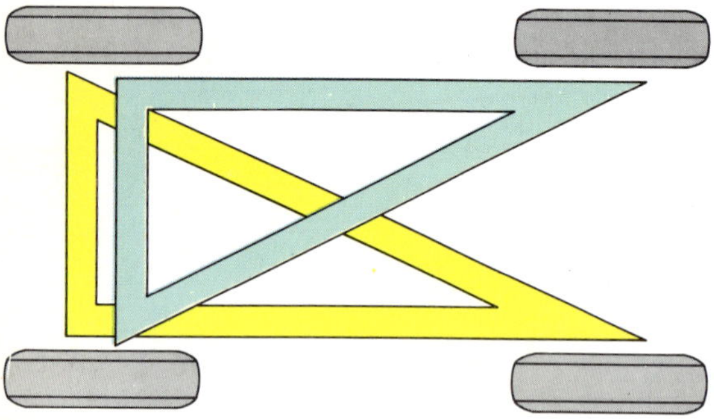

▲ Some cars have two brake systems. If one fails the other can stop the car safely. In the method shown, if one system fails, the brakes still slow three wheels.

Safer and

There are two main ways to make motoring safer. The first, called "active safety", is to build features into cars to make crashes less likely . The second, "passive safety", is to add features that lessen the danger of injury in an accident. One of the most vital aspects of active safety is roadholding. This means the car's ability to remain firmly on the road with the driver fully in control even in difficult conditions. Good brakes play an important part, together with anti-skid tires, firm steering, efficient suspension and a well balanced car. A new idea is to fit several fuel tanks. Pumps automatically spread the fuel between the tanks to balance the car.

Simple points like the comfort of the

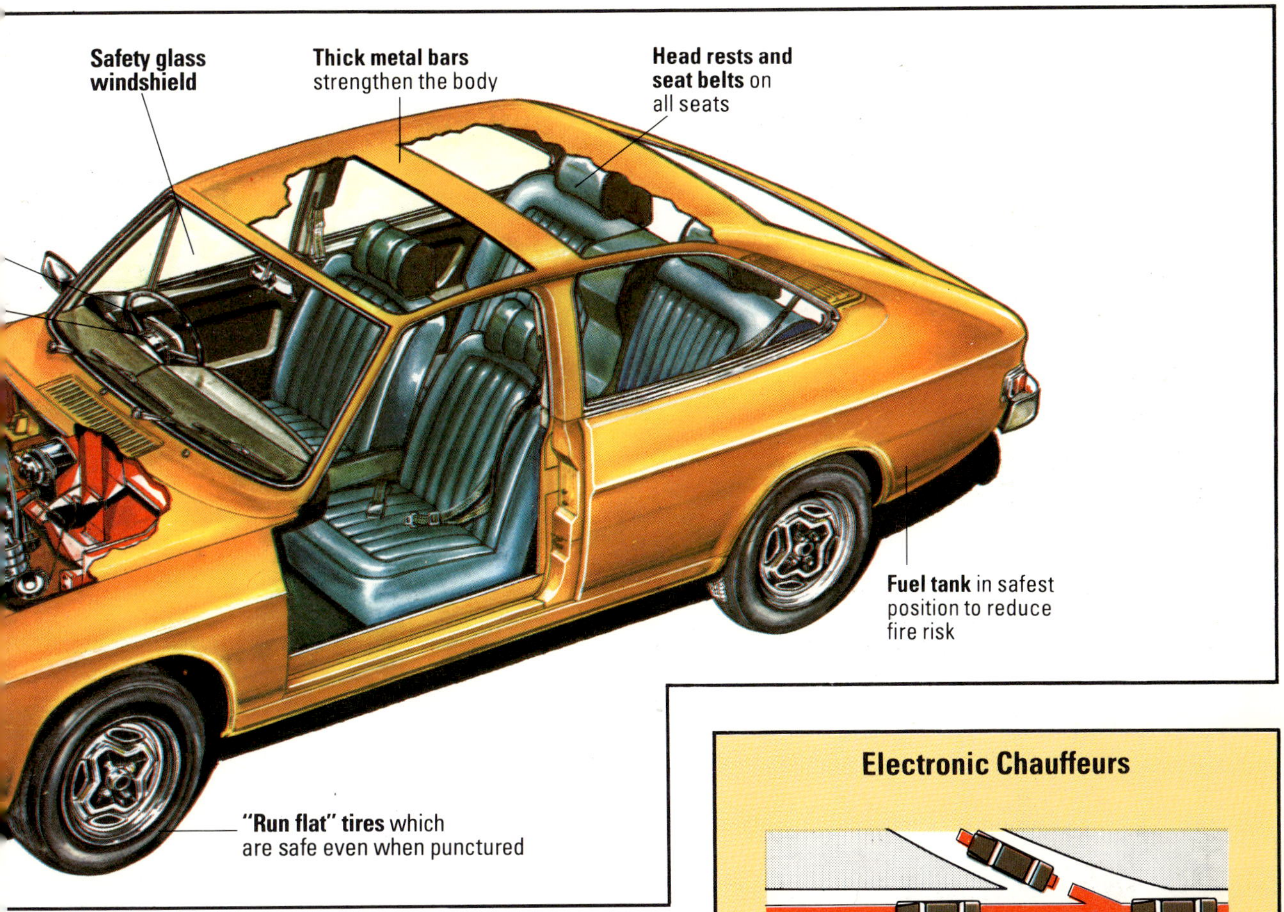

Stronger

driver's seat and the positions of the controls also play a part in active safety. A comfortable driver is more likely to be alert than a stiff one, and can drive more safely if he can reach the controls without taking his hands off the steering wheel. For passive safety, the strength of the actual body is vital. A long bonnet and boot help to cushion the passenger compartment especially if they are fairly weak and the main cab is strengthened with tough metal bars. Designers also make the interior as smooth as possible, and avoid controls and handles which stick out. Features like collapsible steering columns, safety glass, good tires and seat belts are all part of passive safety.

Electronic Chauffeurs

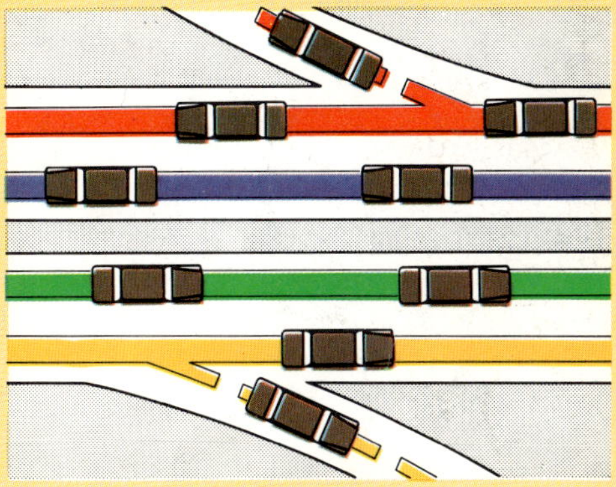

If cars were driven by efficient robots, motoring would be completely safe. One possible system would be to build guideways with wires buried under the road, one for each traffic lane. Electronic signals from the cable are picked up by an "automatic driver" in each car — most ships and airplanes already have "automatic pilots" to keep them on course. Off the guideway the motorist drives the car himself. On reaching the guideway he slots a coded card into a roadside computer to tell it how far he wants to travel. He then hands over to the "electronic chauffer", which drives past computer-controlled traffic lights onto the guideway. Shortly before reaching the planned exit, a buzzer warns the driver to prepare to resume control of the car.

Traffic

Every summer weekend main roads out of cities are jammed with cars. Midweek the streets in city centers are equally choked, and the air is filled with dangerous exhaust fumes. The automobile may be essential to our lives, but the routes of many roads were decided long before the invention of cars.

Super highways are designed for fast long-distance travel by car; but in built-up areas it is often easier to travel by bus or train. Much as we like the freedom of our own cars, motoring can be the most difficult form of travel.

Building better roads would ease the traffic problem but is not always possible. One day the only answer may be to limit the use of the car.

Index

Acknowledgements

Photographs: Cover Ford Motor Company; Endpapers Gerry Cranham; 8 BBC Hulton Picture Library; 13 BBC Hulton Picture Library; 18 Ford Motor Company; 19 Automobiles Peugeot; 20 Volkswagen Ltd.; 21 Citroen Cars Ltd. *left*, BLMC *top right*, General Motors *below right*; 22 Porsche Cars Ltd., Fiat Ltd., Volvo Ltd., Lamborghini Ltd. *left top to bottom*, BLMC *right*; 23 Ford Motor Company, Ferrari Ltd., Jaguar Rover Triumph Ltd. *top to bottom*; 24 Datsun Inc.; 25 Volvo Ltd. *top left*, Ford Motor Company *top right*, Japan Information Service *below right*; 26 Automobiles Peugeot; 27 Ford Motor Company *center*, Rolls Royce Motors Ltd.; 28 Ralph Stein *top*, National Motor Museum *below*; 30-31 United Artists; 32 Goodyear Tire Company *top*, Daily Telegraph Color Library *below*; 32-33 LAT London; 33 NASA; 34 Renault; 35 BBC Hulton Picture Library *left*, Mercedes-Benz Ltd. *right*; 37 LAT London; 38-39 Goodyear Tire Company; 39 Fiat Ltd.; 42 Ford Motor Company; 44 Chicago and North Western Transportation Company *center*, Department of the Environment.

Picture Research: Penny Warn and Jackie Cookson.

Artwork: Michael Trim, Walter Wright, Peter Hutton, Richard Hook, Denis Lord, Edward Hickling, Terry Collins F.S.I.A.